Thoughts, Rants, Poems, some Satire and Crazy Words from my Head # 2

by

Brian Hill

AELIN PUBLISHERS

INDIA

AELIN PUBLISHERS
India

Published by Aelin Publishers India

ISBN 978-81-953782-8-9

www.aelinpublishers.com
Email: aelinpublishers@gmail.com
Instagram/Twitter: aelinpublishers

be astonished by the capable, healthy eyes looking
at you
stop hiding behind the facts
facts, that caring is crucial for survival
we must find a way back to caring and supportive
actions
what happened to us....?

the struggle with opportunity is an interpretation
how do you recognize what is or is not an
opportunity
have you ever thought about this
it's a struggle...

has this year been a hallucination
just like walking into the desert and seeing water
in the distance
what do you see and how do your react
will we be lost in this desert of reality for long...

what, who told you that
I can't believe that happened
no, that's great, isn't it...

your touch is why I survive
the very thought of you makes me smile...

running around in my mind are memories
memories of a meeting chosen
thoughts of your smile drifting towards unknown
eyes
thoughts of you not saying yes to my question
silly question...
will you dance with me...?

it's a dog's life you say
that's not so bad by-the-way
I eat and sleep, poop and pee
love my human, don't you agree
I get to walk and run and roll
and sometimes, ok lots, dig a hole
I love it when I ride in the car
except for when the trip is far
I like to feel my nose in the wind
with my lips a-flapping and making me grin
it's a dog life you say
I can't wait for another day...

today's word is a rant
quiet unfamiliarity is killing us today
how can things, be so misunderstood, by so many
anarchy and lawless mindsets are becoming
increasingly familiar
why
leadership continues to stir it up and never take
ownership
taking ownership, and not pointing to others, is
key in leadership roles
why can't everyone see the problem
please, if you are not recognizing this, and have a
different view
please explain....!
I want to understand
rant over...

memories are the result of past experiences
how far back do they reach
how far into your past do you welcome the
memory
I forget or forgot....whatever...!

the measure of one's self exists in us all
to observe and recognize true nature can be
difficult
to feel and realize how you are seen has its
questions
will you have answers that your true self will listen
to
perhaps you will, but how will you respond
the measure of one's self exists in us all...

as the world sleeps, the enchanting begins
being unseen and quiet, messages are delivered
information bouncing in and about all sleeping
intelligence
apparitions and memories of long-ago actions
as the world awakens, the enchanting flees the
mind
some of the enchanted will recall with faint
impressions
some will remember nothing...

there are roads, streets, paths and trails
there are planes, trains, boats and cars
there is white, black, and all sorts of colors
there is left, right, up and down
there are languages of abundant words
there is rain, sleet, snow, wind, and hail
so many things, so many differences
but to have to decide between right and left
shit is all I got
oh, and there is poop, feces, scat, and dung...

dreams fixed with lost opportunities seem
hopeless
what to do, oh what to do
everyone must remember that dreams occur most
nights
plans can take on different conclusions and survive
we will withstand
we will create a promising future
look up to the sky and see what's ahead in your
dreams...

simplicity will explain the mood of the day
no troubles are coming, they're staying away
I'm spending some time with me and myself
don't get in my way, I'll be back on the twelfth...

the image of Cheeto Face can't be unseen
glaring at us through the tube
spewing forth random worthlessness
infringing on all who watched
how do you undo such nonsense...?

the challenge of the day is to not worry
the solution feels unknown and foreign
attractions and busyness are the best therapy
disturbing as worries are, things change
oh shit, something else to worry about.... :)

when life serves you lemons you make lemonade
when life performs cycles of crazy patterns, you
listen
you listen to the science of reality and truth
you stand up to the certainties that can be
validated
you survive the onslaught of the cycle and wait for
lemons
you make lemonade...

it is time to stand
it is time to let off steam
make time for yourself...

yes, I see it
no, its got to be from the smoke
I know, it does make for some great sunrises and
sets
oh, can you hear the cattle mooing this morning?
makes for peaceful coffee time...

looking back on the novelty of everything I've
written
it's daunting to see how the subject matter changes
our minds live and breathe on what the senses are
provided
can reactions to so much data be influenced
what do you think...?

my mind is marveling at how empty it is for words
to write
have I come to the end of the written trail
I have worried about finding the trails ending
just as the last bend in the path says to finish, I get
a thought
I'm saved
at least for now, and this is what you get today....!

jack and the bat went on a hike
they walked and walked till the nuisance spiked
it's seemed kinda strange to see a bat walking
it doesn't really matter, as they both were just
talking
what in the world could they be talking about
I'm sure it doesn't matter, at least I have doubt
as long as they talk, and talk while they walk
and don't cause trouble as everyone else squawks
there is too much squawking, in the steps of
today's life
we are all very different, so put away that knife
jack and the bat exist only in my mind
if you see something here we must be aligned...

there's a fly in my soup and on somebody's head
how long will it stay there, maybe it's dead
I know I would be dormant if I landed there
right on the top of a lifeless head of hair...

it stole the show, and that is for sure
it stayed and it stayed but wasn't a cure
the words that lured it were truly full of shit
it could only take so much so it left for something
legit...

I'm tired of the conflicts erupting between us all
let's get our act together and answer the needed
call
the politics and policies are in grave need of
revision
why can't we get together to avoid the mad
collision
throw away all the so call facts and see what's
going on
quit throwing your temper into the fray and
creating a nation that's gone...

tension politics
tomorrow we need to vote
we need liberty...

is humanity going to be beautiful again
it has lost its way, and I want to know when
all people of the world, deserve a little break
it has been too long since all of us, really could
partake
mama never told us, there would be days like this
she told us what she knew and would she gave us a
kiss
I want humanity to be beautiful again
let's find a way to save ourselves, and I end, with
an AMEN...

the cowboy slowly enter town riding high on his
horse
the town had no name, he just knew he would find
what he was after
townsfolk seemed to stop in time and stare at his
rugged face
the desert had stolen his youth and good looks
he was a renegade cowboy looking for what
seemed, a friendly face
not sure this town had such a person
this town was not real
this town was a ghost
these folks were in the wind waiting for departure
into the next
he had found Middletown
was he real, was his horse real, where is he
he thought he knew...

the hawk waited for his meal while resting atop
the fence post
gazing intensely at the old dirt road for activity
the storm, that just passed, left a muddy mess for
his prey to splash in
suddenly, from under the gate, he saw movement
a gesture so slight and insignificant that only a
hawk's sharp eyes could see
and see it, he does
slowly, ever so slowly, he begins a slow,
engineered glide, from the post top
swooping in to gracefully capture his target
dinner is served...!

thoughts of your beautiful face penetrate my mind
how can the experience of that moment be genuine
a meeting with so much circumstance
a crossing of paths so real and so seamless
somedays just reach unheard of results
thank you for being there on that day...

waking up this morning I was left between
thoughts
should I or shouldn't I
I took a mental vote and did it
what will you do
when will you do it...?

the darkness of the sky brought it out into view
and my senses
brought out the very brightness of its identity
images used for thousands of year's to navigate
and tell stories
taking man on journeys that even today are a
wonder
I wonder and marvel at the very nature, of nature...

suddenly, silence without any expectations
occurred
being alone with the quite does not have to survive
unattended
silent time can be shared in the best of moments
silent time, even alone, should be pure...

the state of the Union needs to be addressed
it appears to me to be in a big mess
it time to VOTE for one and all
get out there and do it, please answer the call
it's a RIGHT we all have, so please, please VOTE
we can give RISE TO CHANGE, and that is my
quote...

the cleverest of intellect is never orange
what were they thinking when he showed up
strutting around the stage wailing about the
downfall
crying out about how everything needed to change
we were in trouble, or so he said, and some
believed
with a capital T that rhymes with P and that stands
for Politics
please go VOTE
change what has happened, to what should be, and
was...

life is like a patchwork, of various scenes
like the quilt you had, filled with so many things
the colors were bright with patterns mixed up
there were even flowers, sitting in a bright cup
the squares and the shapes made it dizzy to see
they told you a story in patterns of three
life is like that quilt, of patches I suppose
you go, and you go, seeing what life has chose
you never realize what you're about to conceive
just patches of time, are all life is, I believe...

laying in bed waiting, just waiting for 5:55
dawn has arrived
5:55 AM is a reminder that a fresh new day is here
arrived with a gentle call to stretch and welcome
its newness
listen to the sound of coffee grinding and brewing
into your cup
gaze at the morning stars that have been above for
eons
smell the chilled dawn air as you just breath
take a moment and throw your arms up and out
into a large welcoming stretch
and then
noise from morning traffic on Center Street shake
your mood and your awake...

the glory days will start again soon
it's been so long, covered by this cocoon
there is arguing and fighting about the strangest of
things
we can't even hear, the birds when they sing
how did we get here, we all can't be wrong
why are we running, we still have a song
we are in the land, of the brave and the free
let's get back to that, lets all bend a knee...

the reactions we've had to this years differences
are a predicament
they will have an effect for year's to come
friendships lost because of opinions
opinions established by the social dependencies
we retain
the dumbing down of the real news
as we come to the end, be one to pause and reflect
look back and determine where you fit in, in this
spectacle...

it's nearly over
suspicions will fade away
we can dream can't we...

the secret path appeared before us
what is to become of the path behind us...?

man, without wisdom, is uncivilized
understanding how to decide and teach
are we headed backward or forwards
the future, currently exists, only in our minds
do, or will we, have the vision to move
to move past the present, into the future
ouch, (my brain exploded)...

I'm finding it difficult
do you understand
I'm finding it tough
do you see the problem
I'm finding reality hard to find
am I alone in this quandary....?

the world is much better with good friends around
they visit, they chat and the jokes are profound
the world is just better when they are about
you forget that they know what they know, no
doubt
the world has gone silly, and that is just fine
when your friends come to call and share some
good time
thanks to you all, wherever you may be
life would without you, my friends, would be a mad
potpourri...

a pleasant memory of riding in cars
taking us to places so near and so far
looking out the windows in amazement and
wonder
as we pass all the sights that make our minds
ponder
the freeways, the streets, the canyons, and alleys
rolling along at great speeds and right through the
valleys
through the window you see, a whole different
world
as the wheels roll along and the sights are
unfurled...

looking down the dirt road at what lay ahead was
daunting
lucky for us the jeep, and our driver, could handle
it
rocks and lose dirt were about to be challenged
rocking back and forth and moving at a snail's pace
we began
you could hear the bottom of the jeep scraping on
the rocks
you could feel the tension of the driver as he
negotiated the terrain
slowly, we made it through the worst of it
and on to the next...

the Big Horn left his tracks for us to discover
slowly wandering in and out of the wash
wandering about in search of food leaving signs in
the dusty road
we were careful not to disturb these signs so
others could discover...

have you ever seen a Big Horn Sheep
they wander about with nary a peep
they climb on rocks like they're not even there
jump all around without any care
their beauty is amazing, their magnificence divine
just seeing one is lucky and that's by design
be careful and quiet with the chance comes your
way
observing these animals will make for a great day...

the feelings that exist don't seem real
suddenly relief is beginning to rise up
change may be waiting on the other side of the
twisted highway
on the other side...
ON THE OTHER SIDE...

if the barrier suddenly opened up
what would appear in your view
would it be a cleansing for new times
or the continuing of unpleasant news
I would hope for a fresh and welcome world
where society all got along
go back to sanity and reason
and return when the nation was strong...

today's the day, and the future will talk
we all had a choice to give rise to the walk
I hope we all did, what we know we should do
the results will mean, some difference to (who)?
I'm hoping the change will move us along
with a peaceful exchange and a newness that's
strong...!

the secret is simply an illusion in today's world
the mirror into reality has been clouded with haze
we can only hope for a cleansing
cleansing of all and everything, in and behind the
mirror
as we look into it, we crave the truth...

the spirits of our forefathers are turning in their
grave
our land has been home to freedom and liberty for
years
why would we allow the orange fog to control and
suppress that right
our founders fought for and gained that right for us
why would some question, and want that privilege
squashed
is it a reality that has come to stay?
NO, is the only answer here
let our ancestors know that democracy is not in
hiding...

up in the clouds, is where we are
floating around our very own star
how can it be, we ended up here
we are so high and it seems unclear
the world below is all f-ckd up
I'm looking down and it seems corrupt
time will tell if a correction will come
I'll wait up here till my sanity is numb...

I had to get out into the sun
I had to have my eyes see the world
why had it gone the way it did
suddenly, it seemed like we all could breathe
easier
there were no more signs of angst and nervous
hatred
people were getting along
what, was this for real
someone got deflated and whined down history
lane
I can hope, can't I....?

is it too soon, to hope this is true
can I say it now, and share my new view
fogs are lifting and hope is back
the sun will come out and get us on track
if all goes well and unity returns
democracy will follow around the next turn
arguments and yelling will soon be replaced
kindness and friendship should return in great
haste
looking forward to the change in the world we all
know
go out there and help this new message to grow...

the rains came in short, but lovely, bursts
clouds, that had been only skyward visitors,
decided to weep
welcome, welcome rain from high up
come and fill our flowers cup
leave some moisture for us to keep
leave it while the desert sleeps
let it soak into the ground
giving up life's nectar, with nary a sound
the rains came in short, but lovely bursts...

lost happiness is only a myth
try to forget it and see
you'll find it again in seconds
and admit that it's there by decree
it won't be lost forever
if it ever was lost at all
we will all find it right away
and that task is not at all small...

wake up to a new dawn
it's uplifting
see the light of the sun lay down its warmth
it's enlightening
feel the warmth and honor its importance
it's reassuring
have a wonderful day
it's worth it...

another scattered day looking for lost humanity
look behind every rock
look behind every nook
look behind every cranny
think, just think
where would you be, if you were humanity
where would you go, if you lost yourself
look, just look...

what will be lost today
it's the end of the week and we made it through the
chaos
take a minute and review your thoughts
where will next week take you....?

one moment in anger makes you stop and think
number (1) why the anger occurred
number (2) how did you handle it
number (3) did the result do anybody any good
taking time to really understand that moment
when you knew
number (1) you were mad
number (2) you thought you knew why
number (3) you acted without any real emotion
well, not sure where this rant is going, but I feel so
much better
it helps to think it through, doesn't it....?

looking out over the vastness of today, gives me
pause
what's going to happen to change circumstances
is there a conceivable way to ease the pain of
actuality
is it real, or is it viewed from a distance behind a
mirror of fantasy
oh crap
it's another subway of words trying to be written
and understood
what does this mean....?    this
my brain exploded this morning...

what is real today
have we become unseeing
can truth not be seen...

excuse my rant, but
inattentive is the new common
oblivious might be a better word for it
unaware stands strong in the mix
such high standards for us to conquer
can we DO IT....?

vibrations in the early morning air is an awakening
sit back, relax and take it in
take it in with all you got and sip your coffee
take it in and share it throughout the day
early mornings are not everybody's cup of coffee
it's a good alone time for the rest of us....!

the amazing machine we have inside us all
stores and contains information from all sources
makes decisions so rapidly that even computers
get left behind
tells us when we are happy, hurt, loved, tired,
hungry and so many more
creates wonders that yesterday, were truly, just a
wonder
how can this machine be controlled by such awful
outside sources
sources that split families, crush dreams and take
away our democracy
PEOPLE, we need to stop this negative fuel
bombarding our brains...

there once was a land that was rich with things
everything working with no broken swings
about 4 years ago it started to fail
the spirit of the nation was turning quite pale
some thought it was good and just went along
others were appalled and knew it was wrong
what was the reason many of us asked
it appears that our rights are questioned and
tasked
we rambled about and fought from within
losing some friends and a few of our kin
we need this to change we said in a vote
but the man at the top, he started to gloat
he ate up the laws and turned into a grinch
casting people about and not giving an inch
we elected in another to take on the task
to cast the grinch out and peel off his mask
well grinch wouldn't budge and sent out his saps

to alter results and further the collapse
what do we do, can we take on more shit
I for one am just done, and the grinch has to quit...

it seems Prez Grinch has met his match
most people agree he needs to dispatch
it want be long before our man Joe steps in
and cleans up the mess that was not a win-win
I'm told, that in history, this story will reign
I'm hoping we learn from all the insane
let's learn to be forgiving and get back our pride
and try to all be, on at least the same side
I love this great country but hate where it's been
can we all just agree, at least try to begin....?
well, Prez Grinch has decided that to lose is to succeed
how can this happen in the land of the freed

I don't suggest that we go back in time
yet this practice is wrong and a really big crime
go back to a time when the country was strong
I think you will see how this practice is wrong
he lost and he needs to exit the seat
give our Joe some relief as he takes on the heat....!

yes, oh yes, it's really quite real
President Grinch has lost his appeal
he's changed up his color to try to blend in
it really won't work because of his skin
it's really not orange, I think it's fake red
he's having some trouble getting this through his
head
he can't believe, that he surely didn't win
he's throwing some tantrums that make us all spin
when, oh when, will this torture be through
it will make room for changes and let us renew....!

it seems Prez Grinch, has a job to commit
it's that time of year, we have to admit
turkey pardoning is indeed a big thing
Prez Grinch just loves it as he thinks he's a king
the turkey is chosen and brought to the garden
it struts and it clucks and Prez says "your
pardoned"...

(I was ask by folks to try and detect
some good that Prez did. They said I
refused to see any good. That's not true
I have tried but this is my
response......)

I can't refuse to see what's not there
Unless it's sitting in an unseen chair
What is it, that you can see
I see a man that is truly a flea
A flea that sucks the air out of us
A flea that exists that we cannot trust
A flea that really should be gone
A flea who's use just makes us yawn
What about this flea do you see
What about this flea makes you free....?